Library of Congress Cataloging-in-Publication Data

Holmes, Margaret M. , 1944
Sam's dad died : a child's book of hope through grief / by
Margaret Holmes with Sasha Mudlaff :
illustrated by Susan Aitken.
p.16.cm.
Summary: After his father dies, Sam tells how he feels and what he can do so he doesn't hurt so much.
ISBN: 1-56123-123-1
1. Grief in children--juvenile literature. 2. Bereavement in children--Juvenile literature. 3. Fathers--Death--Psychological aspects--Juvenile literature. 4. Children and death--Juvenile literature. (1. Death. 2. Grief. 3. Fathers and sons.)
I. Mudlaff, Sasha J., 1967-
II. Aitken, Susan, ill.
III. Title.
BF723.G75H68 1999
155.9'37--dc21

98-46213
CIP
AC

Centering Corporation
PO Box 4600
Omaha, NE 68104

Phone: 402-553-1200
Fax: 402-553-0507

www.centering.org

Sam's Dad Died

A Child's Book of Hope Through Grief

By Margaret M. Holmes
Afterward by Sasha J. Mudlaff, M.A.
Illustrated by Susan Aitken

In memory of my father,
Walter C. Mehne
He gave me so many good feelings to keep inside of me.

My name is Sam. My real name is Samuel Jay Sullivan, Jr. That was my dad's name too. He said my name has junior at the end so people would know I am his son. My dad used to tell me a lot of stuff. He died and I miss him so much.

I have so many questions and I wonder about so many things. I sure wish I could talk to Daddy. I worry about asking too many questions. I am afraid I will make someone else sad.

When Mommy and I talk about Daddy, we cry and hug each other. We say how much it hurts. Sometimes when we talk about Daddy we laugh and remember funny stories. I feel better when we talk about Daddy. Maybe it is good for everyone when we talk.

After my dad died I wanted to be just like him. I tried to do things like he used to do, but it was just too hard. Other times I wanted to be a baby. I thought that would be a lot easier. I have decided it is best for me just to be me. My mom says that helps the most.

I feel different now. Like part of me is missing. Billy McIntyre's father died, too. Billy says it feels like there is a big hole in his chest and everyone can see it. I feel that way too. I am sorry Billy is sad. But I am glad to have a friend like him.

There are many changes. I wish things could be the way they were. Sometimes I get really angry. I just have to let my feelings out. I feel better after that. Crying helps, too. Sometimes I feel so sad, I don't know what else to do. Once in a while the tears just slip out and I don't really know why. It is embarrassing when that happens. I try not to do it, but when I do it is okay.

It seems as if school is harder for me now. There is so much to think about. It feels like my brain is too full to learn new things. I have to try very hard to do my best. I am proud of myself when I do and that makes me feel better.

I have found a special place where I can be by myself. It feels nice to be alone. The quiet seems soft–like a warm fuzzy blanket.

Most of the time I play with my friends. We pretend to be astronauts or soldiers or kings. We like to run and play games. We do a lot of things. Laughing is the best. When I laugh I don't hurt as much. My Dad would be happy about that.

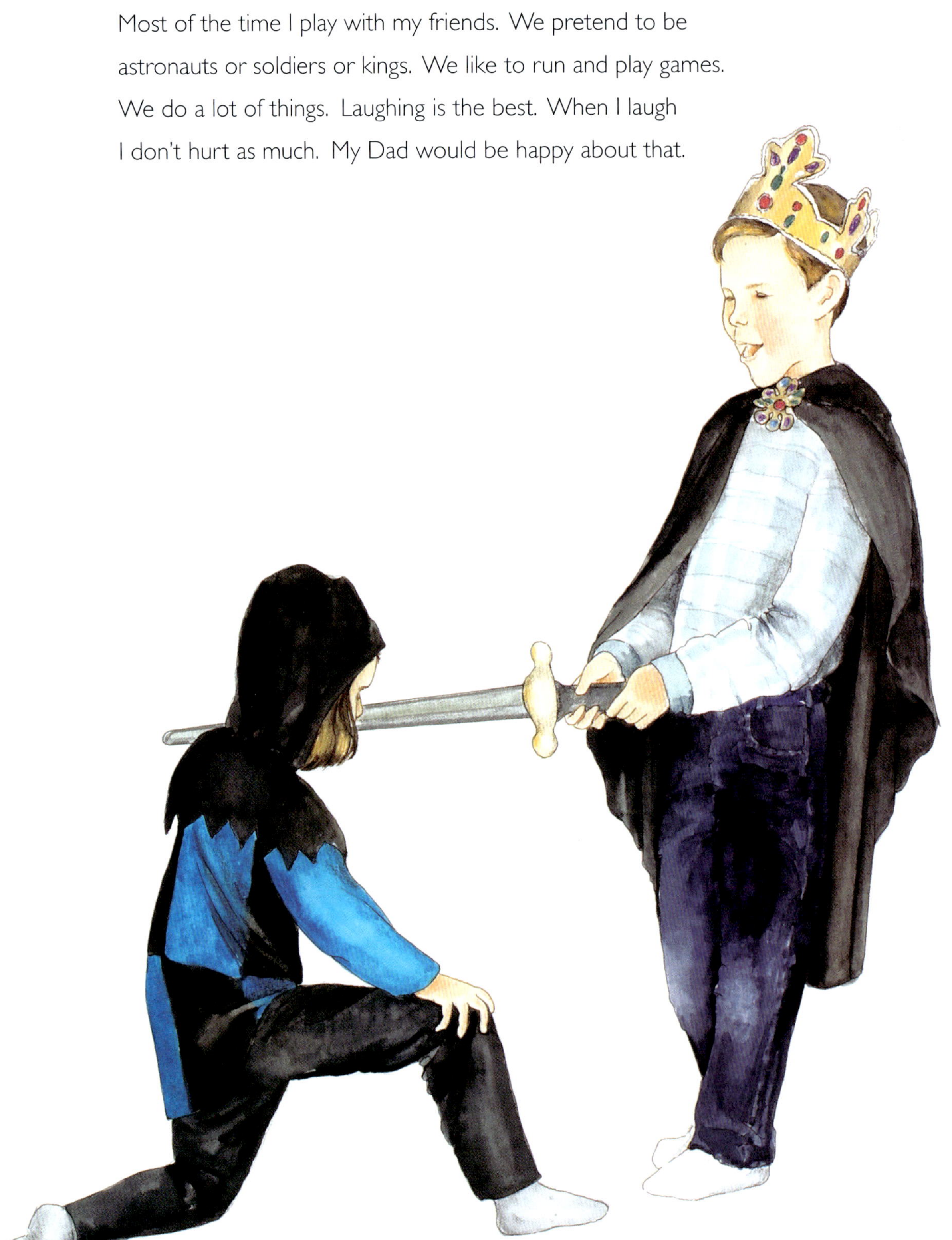

I really loved my dad. It felt so good to be with him. When I was with daddy I didn't worry so much. I felt strong and brave. I felt funny and smart. I felt loved. I am glad he gave me so many good feelings to keep inside of me. I remember those feelings and I love him still. I know I always will.

A special note to caregivers from Sasha

No child is too young to grieve. When someone loved dies, it has a profound impact, no matter what the child's age or developmental understanding of death may be. There are unique grief issues to consider for the child whose parent has died. Our hope is that this book be used as a tool to facilitate communication and conversation between a caring adult and the child about the grief they are currently experiencing.

The following is a list of important things to consider when dealing with a grieving child. Many of these issues are touched upon in the story:

The death of someone loved, especially that of a parent, shakes a child's sense of security. Often the next overwhelming thought is, "Is my other parent going to die, too?" If so, "Who will take care of me?" Clingy or regressive behavior is very common for the first weeks or months following the death.

It is very important to attempt to maintain the child's daily routine if at all possible. This continuity helps provide the child with some sense of security and stability during a time of uncertainty.

Other losses often accompany the identified loss. A change in residence, caretaker, school or peer group, are secondary losses which can complicate the primary loss.

Grieving children are very sensitive and perceptive as well as protective of those around them. They may decide not to express their grief openly because they do not want to risk "making mommy or daddy cry."

Children need an outlet for their feelings. There are many appropriate methods of expression: talking, crying, writing, drawing, sports, punching a pillow, etc.

A child's questions should be answered as directly and honestly as possible, even if the answer is "I don't know." This expresses your respect toward the child and the very real feelings he or she is experiencing. Children tend to know when they aren't being told the whole truth; sometimes the answers they will come up with in their own minds are much more frightening than the truth.

Children who have experienced the death of a parent, often feel very different from their peers–that somehow they even look different to others now. A child's self-esteem is greatly affected as he or she sometimes assumes they are the only one on earth who have had a parent die. Being around other children who have experienced a similar loss can facilitate healing.

Be certain that the child is still expected to abide by "the rules." It is important that rules and discipline are still enforced at home–this will help to stabilize the child's sense of security, which has been threatened by the death of a parent.

Grief causes difficulty in concentration. Children may experience a shortened attention span, and school work can be affected. It is important that a teacher be informed about any loss a child is enduring.

Encourage the child's thoughts, discussions, or creativity in terms of his or her memories of the person who has died. This helps the child to understand and have hope that even though someone has died they will continue to live within our hearts forever.

About the Author

Margaret Holmes' first writing projects were for her daughter's Sunday School class, which led to writing the stories for a Sunday School Curriculum.

Margaret continued to write children's picture books with an emphasis on books to help children cope with problems. She has published an article in an academic journal describing the process of writing bibliotherapy books for young children. Margaret has three children's picture books in print. Two of them have been selected outstanding by the Parent Council.

She lives with her husband, John, in Pleasant Hill, IA. They have two grown daughters, Sarah and Katie and one granddaughter, Emma Josephine.

Afterward by Sasha Mudlaff

Sasha J. Mudlaff is the grief consultant for Hamilton's Academy of Grief & Loss as well as Hospice of Central Iowa in Des Moines where she specializes in work with grieving children. She received her undergraduate degree in psychology from Cornell College in Mt. Vernon Iowa and her master's degree in developmental psychology from Columbia University in New York.

She and her husband Michael (pastor of Westkirk Presbyterian Church in Urbandale) live in Clive with their three boys Micah, Johan and Nathanael and their fourth child due to be born in August of 2005. During this season of her life she is thoroughly enjoying being a stay-at-home mom while working from her home.

About the Illustrator

Susan is an art educator, watercolorist and home schooling mom to four children. She has been illustrating for Centering Corporation for many years. She counts it a privilege to be able to help children as they attempt to cope with the death of a loved one.